Show Me Your Smile!

A Visit to the Dentist

by Christine Ricci
illustrated by Robert Roper

SCHOLASTIC INC.
New York   Toronto   London   Auckland   Sydney
Mexico City   New Delhi   Hong Kong   Buenos Aires

Based on the TV series *Dora the Explorer*® as seen on Nick Jr.®

ISBN 0-439-72385-X

12 11 10 9 8 7 6 5 4 3 2 1   5 6 7 8 9 10/0

Printed in the U.S.A.   23

First Scholastic printing, February 2005

¡Hola! I'm Dora! I'm going to the dentist's office to have my teeth cleaned today. Have you ever been to the dentist?

I have to wait for my turn with the dentist. The waiting room has lots of things to do. I want to color a picture. Do you see some crayons?

crayons

The dental assistant is calling my name. It's my turn! Will you come with me into the dentist's office? Great! Let's go! *¡Vámonos!*

Wow! Look at all the neat things! There's a big chair that goes up and down. Do you see a light? The dentist needs a light to see inside my mouth. What else do you see in the dentist's room?

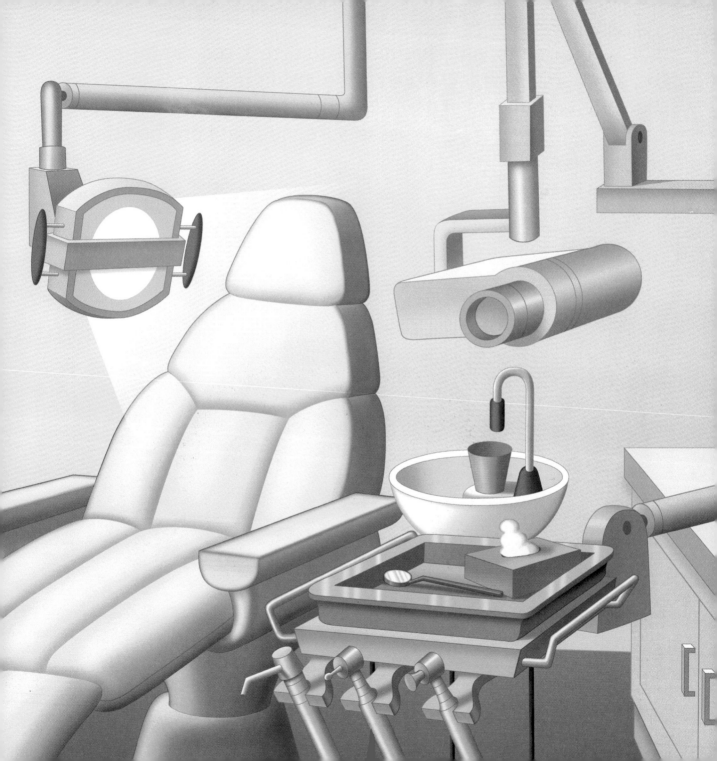

Now it's time for the dental assistant to X-ray my teeth. The X ray will show a picture of the inside of my mouth. It shows all my bones and my teeth. The dentist can look at it to make sure my teeth are healthy.

The dental assistant covers me with a heavy apron. Then I have to sit very still for the camera. When the camera goes *click,* the X ray is done!

Can you find the X ray of my teeth? Who else had their teeth X-rayed at the dentist's office?

Here comes the dentist! She uses special tools to check and clean my teeth.

Do you see the tool with a circle on the end of it? It's a mirror for your mouth! The dentist uses it to see all the hidden areas around your teeth. The tool with a hook on the end is called an *explorer*. The dentist uses it to explore your teeth. Hey, the dentist is an explorer just like me!

I need to open my mouth really wide, so the dentist can check my teeth. Can you open your mouth really wide? Great! Open wide! *¡Abre!*

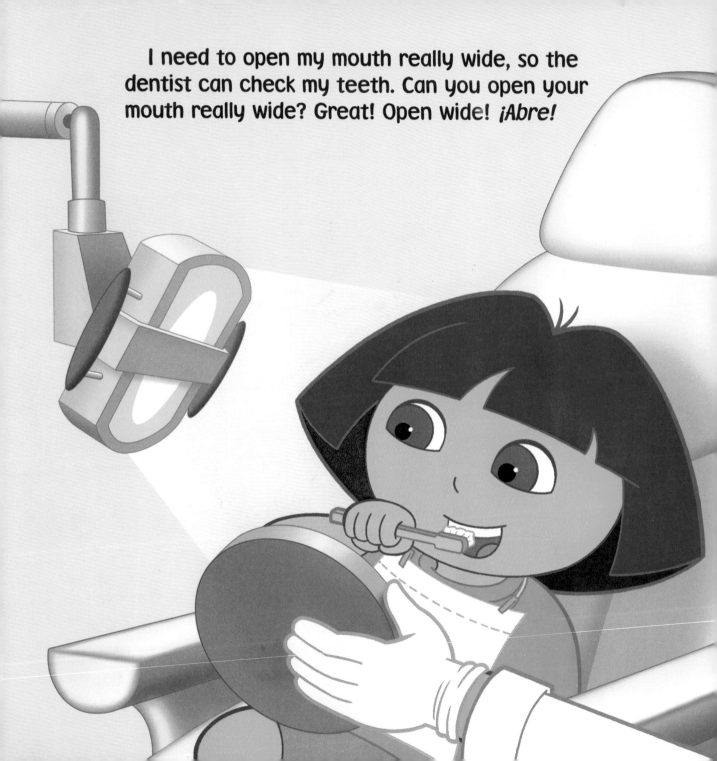

First the dentist cleaned my teeth with a special tool. Now she is showing me how to brush my teeth with a toothbrush. The dentist says I should brush after breakfast and again before bedtime.

Time to floss my teeth! The dentist takes a long piece of waxy string called dental floss and wiggles it between my teeth. She says that I should have my *mami* help me floss every night to make sure that the spaces between my teeth stay clean.

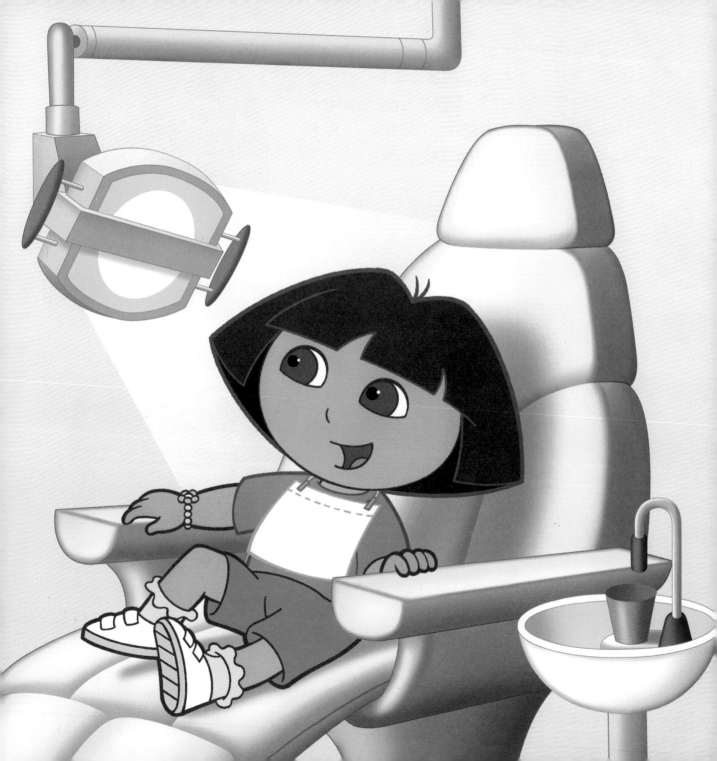

The dentist checked my X ray
and found a cavity in my mouth.
A cavity is a little hole in a tooth.
The dentist needs to fill the cavity,
so it doesn't get any bigger.

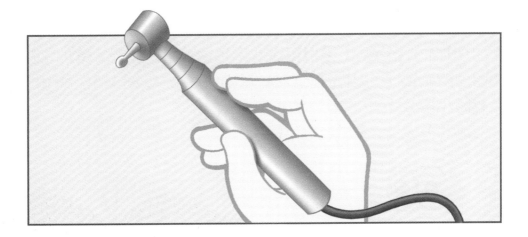

She uses a tool to get my tooth ready for the filling. It makes a funny *whirrrrrring* sound as it spins around and around. Then the dentist fills the hole. Now my tooth is all better! All my teeth feel shiny and new!

I was such a good patient! The dentist is letting me pick out a new toothbrush and a sticker. I love stars! Do you see the star sticker? My favorite color is purple. Can you find the purple toothbrush?

Oh, no! I hear Swiper the fox! He'll try to swipe the stickers and toothbrushes. If you see Swiper, say "Swiper, no swiping!"

Yay! We stopped
Swiper.
Swiper will get
his very own sticker
and toothbrush after
the dentist cleans
his teeth!

¡Excelente! Now I have bright, clean, shiny teeth.
Going to the dentist makes me want to SMILE!
Show me your smile!
Good smiling! We did it!